YOUR KNOWLEDGE HAS VALUE

- We will publish your bachelor's and
  master's thesis, essays and papers

- Your own eBook and book -
  sold worldwide in all relevant shops

- Earn money with each sale

Upload your text at www.GRIN.com
and publish for free

Bibliographic information published by the German National Library:

The German National Library lists this publication in the National Bibliography; detailed bibliographic data are available on the Internet at http://dnb.dnb.de .

This book is copyright material and must not be copied, reproduced, transferred, distributed, leased, licensed or publicly performed or used in any way except as specifically permitted in writing by the publishers, as allowed under the terms and conditions under which it was purchased or as strictly permitted by applicable copyright law. Any unauthorized distribution or use of this text may be a direct infringement of the author s and publisher s rights and those responsible may be liable in law accordingly.

Imprint:

Copyright © 2016 GRIN Verlag, Open Publishing GmbH
Print and binding: Books on Demand GmbH, Norderstedt Germany
ISBN: 978-3-668-16156-6

This book at GRIN:

http://www.grin.com/en/e-book/316856/de-colonial-thoughts-de-linking-epistemo-logy-rethinking-contemporaneity

Sayan Dey

De-colonial Thoughts. De-linking Epistemology, Rethinking Contemporaneity and De-colonizing the Screen

Three Essays

GRIN Publishing

GRIN - Your knowledge has value

Since its foundation in 1998, GRIN has specialized in publishing academic texts by students, college teachers and other academics as e-book and printed book. The website www.grin.com is an ideal platform for presenting term papers, final papers, scientific essays, dissertations and specialist books.

Visit us on the internet:

http://www.grin.com/

http://www.facebook.com/grincom

http://www.twitter.com/grin_com

De-colonial Thoughts: An Essay-ntial Triumvirate

Index

Preface

The book "De-colonial Thoughts: An Essay-ntial Triumvirate" took birth in my mind when I have three essays which explore three different perspectives of de-coloniality but they connect to each other with the underlying theme. It conceives a major section of my thoughts and ideas associated with the element of de-coloniality and hope it will be of great help for the scholars who are venturing new to this field.

De-linking Epistemology: Unlearning to Relearn

Vidyā Dadāti Vinayaṁ Vinayād Yāti Pātratām|
Pātratvāddhanamāpnoti Dhanāddharmaṁ Tataḥ Sukham

(Knowledge gives humility, from humility one attains character
From character one acquires wealth, from wealth good deeds,
Follows then happiness)

The above mentioned adage has been imbibed from an ancient Indian text which applauds the universal constructive quality of knowledge and its system. Since ages the globe has undergone multi-dimensional geopolitical shifts largely motivated by the exertion and channelizing of power across and over. The world has consistently been invaded by different segments of political thoughts and ideas since the pre-colonial times and has largely been maneuvered through different violent tactics but the epistemological insurgence and influence can never be left ignored. Michel Foucault in his seminal essay *Discipline and Punish: The Birth of Prison* philosophizes:

> "There is no power relation without the correlative constitution of a field of knowledge, nor any knowledge that does not presuppose and constitute at the same time power relations."

(Focault, *Discipline and Punish: The Birth of Prison*)

Power and Knowledge indeed exists in symbiosis with each other and it has been variously defined by intellectuals across the world. The formats and designs of power execution across ages varies from one place to another in terms of the *nomos* within which a society or community is confined but the system of knowledge plays functions as the central motivational force towards formulating and executing the multifarious theoretical and philosophical compartmentalization like pre-colonial, colonial, postcolonial, anti-colonial or de-colonial.

There has been endless controversies and debates associated with the execution of these terms which has undergone endless redefinitions and manipulations with respect to individual or collective discourses. I have always felt strongly that the entire grammar of our existence and pursuance is largely influenced by the entangled system of knowledge execution which encapsulates us entirely. The global establishment and the dissemination of knowledge is a highly conflicting premise through which multidimensional thoughts interact, debate and lead to the production of brand new ideologues. But in the current era of high capitalism, where the entire society floats over the endless sea of simulated productions entangled with in its cobweb of confusions it is very difficult to recognize and signify the individual premises of knowledge production system in terms of respective communities, class, religion or the if in the Indian perspective we say then obviously caste is an peculiar quotient in our socio-cultural system. The phrase 'global knowledge' is itself manifested with severe controversies because what we today discourse or practice as global is local Eurocentric conceptualization which were appropriated, experimented and quite successfully over and across different corners of the globe.

The appropriation of the Eurocentric epistemology has been globally emancipated through the colonial lines of thoughts which were propelled through seduction and psychological manipulation over the societies and cultures that did not experience the so called enlightenment of modernization. Historical records reveal that during the 14th century, under the supervision of the church, different European nations undertook their respective civilizing mission towards the west (i.e. Americas and Caribbean) to discover and invent a new world which will serve their various industrial and economic needs. After a few centuries the same thing was experienced by the eastern part of the globe.

In fact, the cartographical representation that we are all habituated with is none other than the product of the colonial episteme. Pre-colonial geography was two dimensional – space and time. The scriptural prospect of interpretation was partially absent from their culture and discourse was largely depended on the natural shifts and turnovers rather than the infected human scriptures. If we pervade into the world of Incas and Aztecs who played an integral part towards the formulation of the traditional Latin American Culture we find a different world altogether which are not segmented with nations, states or unions. The world doesn't appear to so finely segment and the Mayan civilization which persisted across most parts of the present South American continent have represent the entire Americas in a very prominent way. Shifting our focus towards the other part the world, it is quite astonishing that Europe has been awarded a very indistinguishable position which is totally paradoxical in the present scenario. The European continent of the eastern side of the map appears to be in a very confused state and seems to be a pinprick amongst the vast continents.

With the passage of time this cartographical structure was expropriated by Spanish and the French who physically invaded, interrupted and exploited the geographical structures but epistemologically they colonized the entire continent. I think it is at this moment Europe began to expand its tentacles more ideologically rather than physically, across the globe and it is also the same 'ideological' continent with its wide abyss of episteme reins the world. Usually the educational institutes, especially within the 'Third World Nations' (which is again a Eurocentric construct!) usually interprets colonialism rather to be apt misinterprets the term within the perspectives of politics. But before embarking on political expansions Europe unleashed its colonial design through its highly manipulative discourse which widely appealed to the 'uncivilized mass' who lingered in utter darkness. My paper basically looks forward to identify the possibilities of how in the present global scenario we can look forward to avail the various options through which we can de-link epistemology from the clutches of the ongoing westernization through unlearning and then relearning. It does sound a bit weird but in order to re-think and re-interpret the globe it is crucial for us to reflect back to the roots of the issues rather than swarming objectively.

According to me this very process should enunciate through disrupting the linear mode of interpreting our existence in the most non-linear fashion. In the language of eminent Chilean biologist Humberto Maturana (who used it though in a different context), we have to 'step out' of our present matrix of experience, travel back and 'step in' within the possible dimensionalities of various de-colonial options that are available for us. I have quite been conscious and in few cases I should rather say over-conscious with my grammatical usage while drafting my paper so that in no ways I am convicted over the charges of self-contradiction. The biggest postmodern debate, besides everything has been to accept or to reject history. But the premise of history is itself highly disputed because it has been tampered, intersected and reinterpreted from time to time. Our primary initiative should be to disentangle history from the garbs of totalitarianism, excavate, identify and preach the individual 'his-stories' or 'her-stories' that has been deliberately left dormant by and within the faction of the knowledge system that is globally articulated. With respect to this, I would like to inculcate the concept of 'border thinking' or 'border epistemology' through Arturo Escobar's essay *Worlds and Knowledges Otherwise* which he propagated as the crucial juncture which we should all explore in order to embark on our goal. In the very introductory part of his paper, Escobar declares:

"The present paper focuses on a 'border' that is gaining salience in recent years, particularly as a result of the work of an increasingly interconnected group of researchers in Latin America and United States with smaller branches elsewhere. I am referring to the concepts of 'border thinking' and 'border epistemologies' associated with a larger effort that I will call here the 'modernity/coloniality research program.'"

(Escobar:2)

The central motive towards introducing the modernity/coloniality research program is to divulge away from the postmodern dependency theories on common modern narratives based on a few institutional propagandas like Christianity, liberalism or Marxism. In order to rethink the entire episteme of existence it is for us to realize and explore the 'non-Eurocentric modes' of thinking. I have always wondered why is it every time necessary that whenever we are referring nay new forms of theoretical or philosophical establishments we have to consider the west. Will it be ever possible for us to disrupt this traditional ideological reference line of moving from west to east and inherit the opposite? These questions continues to haunt my mind and this paper can also be termed as my quest to seek certain possibilities with these questions. Now I would also like to clarify that when I am referring to the terms like 'delinking' or 'unlearning' I am not of the view to move outside the colonial or in the present aspect neo-colonial premise to create a new epistemological unity. Our primary task is to unearth the history that has created us in order to de-establish the history that has simply embellished the modern discourse premise. And my journey starts from India.

India has undergone a stringent perigesis from the pre-colonial through the colonial drainage across and into the postcolonial framework. India has always been mapped or rather trafficked to the west under several occidental phrases like the nation of 'snake charmers', market for 'pot bellied money minded brainless *seths*' and women has been presented as 'innocent seductresses.' But India is the only nation in the world we all know with such unified yet diversified socio-cultural norms and traditions. The nation 'India' is actually a colonial construct and to the ancient world it has always been known as 'Bharat' or the 'Maha-Bharat' or the Great India. The above mentioned terminology was never in terms of vast geographical or geo-political expanses harnessed by the respective kingdoms within or outside the nation. Bharat or to be more precise the ideological Bharat evolved from a vast galaxy of enriching indigenous ideological premises free from the toxic garb of totalitarianism and hegemony. The occidental-oriental encounter has mostly been characterized by the encounter between science and religion. Yes Indeed, like many other 'Third-World' societies Bharat proudly accommodated and practiced Theo-centrism. Infact before the sudden outburst of theories and philosophies in the second half of the 19th century, the global society was largely steered by Theo-centric ideologues.

India's epistemological contribution towards the evolution of society and culture has always been embroidered with the very unique balance of divine logic which permeated beyond its strict religious performatives towards other distinguished spheres of knowledge. Unlike Europe where religion from its utter sublime aesthetics transformed itself into a socio-political hegemonic institution when propagation of divine knowledge was no more pursued towards eternal transformations of humans but rather for the sake of achieving politico-economic goals. I deliberately switched over from the perspectives of history towards religion across every nation religion and histories are symbiotic towards each other. Though perennially our historical richness has continuously been intervened with communal conflicts especially the age old Hindu-Muslim psycho-war which often takes a bloody makeover is nothing new to us.

In order to look for its roots we often refer to the India-Pakistan or Indo-Bangladesh border dispute that treacherously truncated one large nation into three parts towards the end of the colonial era, but its roots takes us back to 12th century with the Arab Naval Expeditions which gradually got distributed through their successors – Rashidun Caliphate, Umayyads, Ghaznavids, Delhi Sultanate and obviously the Mughal Empire. But before these foreign intrusions Indian history hardly have any records of massive communal conflicts rather it promotes an exclusive plethora of unified progression in field of art, aesthetics, literature, science, mathematics and technology. Indian history and religion has always been very ambivalent. Before I further proceed I would like to bring to your notice that I am not talking of the monarchial or the typical political history that the ancient scriptures or the engravings are adorned with but the multifarious miniscule yet rich perspectives of history which has been left subjugated from the pre-colonial into the colonial as well in the post-colonial chimera.

The Indian *Vedas, Puranas, Upanishadas* and their multifarious sub-versions are pregnant with endless evidences with well outlined instances about the kaleidoscopic structure of the Indian socio-religious system. The epistemological involvement and transgression of the Indian socio-cultural matrix can be very well defined in terms of Maturana's concept of 'Organism and Niche.' In his book *Tree of Knowledge: The Biological Roots of Human Understanding* biologist Humberto Maturana speaks about how the functionability of the human body also massively contributes towards establishing and preserving social connectivity. Maturana is of the view that like the human body, the society is a large structure which is interconnected with neural elements which are referred to as *niches* and they are both interconnected and trans-connected from one point to another but their point of origin remains very distinctive. This is how actually the nervous system functions within us.

But ideologically it has long been disrupted by the intrusion of totalitarian perspectives that have not only simply impressed themselves into our psyche but also have disrupted the usual indigenous ingredients that lies beneath the making of Indian culture and traditions or rather altogether our very existence in and out of the border. Our biggest drawback is that we fail to distinguish between the experience, perception and illusions. Infact, on the broader perspective the Occidents and the Orients have dissected themselves on the basis of illusion and experience but they function within the same trust. It is this trust which also characterizes the colonizer-colonized relationship which our history often ignores. Eminent postcolonial scholar Dr. Homi K. Bhabha in his essay *Of Mimicry and Man: The ambivalence of colonial discourse* in the book *The Location of Culture* eludes the high ambivalence that persist not only between the colonizer-colonized relationship but also the process that as undertaken by the colonizers to appropriate their forms of history, cultures and heritage either by distempering or by razing the indigenous ones. Despite of India's own socio-cultural why do we continue to take pride in the works of James Mills' *History of India* or E.M. Forster's *Passage to India* which are nothing more than partial observations of Indian manners and morals?

The colonizer-colonized relationship exist on the yardstick of mutual violence in which the both the natives and the outsiders agree upon inheriting new cults and manners replacing the existing ones. But if we look into our history or rather the history of religion as outlined by the texts and the traditional law books, then we find that we have been the continuous victim of misinterpretation since ages. This obviously doesn't mean that everything exist in an unusual utopic balance. Infact the class and caste conflicts forms an integral part of our society intercepted with multilayered gender issues as well. The *Laws of Manu* which is regarded as the traditional book for Indian socio-political and religious system is manifested with such dogmatic pleasures which reject all forms of logic and reason in the garbage bin. But a mere narrow-minded discourse or a few dogmatic practices cannot be used as the metonymy to describe an entire nation in the global episteme. Every culture and traditions encompass an entire living existence comprising of both human and the nature. The largest creative contribution of modernization is bridging the gap between illusion and reality.

While conducting a two week course work at English and Foreign Language University, Shillong in of his class's Argentine semiotician Dr. Walter Mignolo philosophized, 'Illusions makes us live in a valid modern world experience of what we see, think, touch, hear and believe. Illusion is the belief.' The present global epistemological structure within which we are functioning is a product of a world minority of capitalists that has weaved a measureless kingdom of illusion which is continuously been channelized through its massive corpus of tributaries and distributaries to seduce the majority in its gigantic commercial propagandism. It is this numerical minority which forms the current ideological, epistemological majority across and over the globe. Once in the very same course work I was having a chat with Princeton University Professor Simon Gikandi from Kenya and he gave a thought provoking statement against my question, 'Despite so much of indigenous developments in the premises of theory and philosophy why still India lingers under the massive burden of the western ideologies? He started his reply with rectifying me, 'India has not been presented but trafficked in the west.'

The Universe was created so that in an interconnectivity and trans-connectivity with each other which was also represented by the 'Organism and Niche' model of Maturana. But the distinctive points of origination and transfusion are blurred with the insurgence of global ideological packages. India epitomizes a vast legacy of scientific, technological and several mathematical developments which were and is still being largely practiced by the developed nations of the world. Recently the scientists have discovered that the sun which centers our galaxy produces a consistent sound which almost sounds similar like the 'Om' which is the ultimate source of divine power according to the Indian mythology. During the ancient times historical records and independent scriptures note that the ancient priests and sages who have successfully moved beyond the physical shadow line of existence through severe penance have gained 'Om' the ultimate power from the sun. Thus, in the present scenario the Indian version of divine origin of the universe or rather the entire galaxy finely merges with the discourse of western science.

Several mathematical concepts which the major technological and scientific discoveries ride upon have its origin in the ancient lands of India. Speaking about the variegated form of history in art and aesthetics especially in performing arts India underwent disastrous transgression when during the pre-colonial times the monarchial conflicts which encouraged the communal riots often attained the worst shape by dissolving several cultural and social norms and architectural wonders which could have existed as the witness of the Indian history. In case of performative art suppose we take the instance of theatre in which India is blessed with such multifarious forms of theatre and theatrical spectacles based on different classes, communities, religions and genders. Indian theatre is majorly divided into urban and rural theatre, but if our exploration stops over these objective discriminations then we are totally caught in the wrong side. We have different versions of rural and urban theatres like the folk theatre, tribal theatre, street theatres, open air theatres, court plays of the ancient times and many more.

Theatre and performtives in India are not exclusively limited within the periphery of stage enactments but also it transcends beyond and into other forms like dance-theatre or musical theatre imbibed with its own uniqueness. The significance in theatrics lies largely towards shaping the Indian epistemological structure which was never in need of the western touch. The eastern part of the world including the regions of Africa oral traditions played a pivotal role towards formulating the indigenous culture and knowledge system. From the grandma folk tales of our childhood, the jabberwocky rhymes of Bengali poet Sukumar Ray (*Abol-Tabol*), through the *Abolkara* tradition of Orissa into the fables of *Panchatantra*. When the world celebrates the western allegories of Jonathan Swift (for *Gulliver's Travels* we Indians have our own knowledge platform.

Western Knowledge is onto-theological. Prior to the arrival of Jacques Derrida it was god centered which he transformed it as logo-centric. This theology was hierarchal and this hierarchy is still ensured in the western knowledge system. Indian knowledge system detests any forms of hierarchy during the pre-colonial times and it has always existed on the horizontal plane. Divine knowledge which has pervaded into every perspectives of the Indian epistemic existence has always searched for the self, the knowledge of the self. The domain of Indian knowledge is pluriversal within which every perspectives of expression find a space rather than universalizing a few exploitative versions of pre-notion institutional preaching. Our cultural consciousness has been characterized with two knowledge worlds – scriptural and folk. Folk traditions which were mostly expropriated during the colonial times in order suppress and dislodge the national indigenous quality, deconstructed the whole theses of global divine knowledge propagated through Christianity.

The folk world doesn't have a god at the center. It has a supreme creator who is a spirit and is a very ambivalent character who persists within the human civilization. The traditional Indian knowledge system never ever distinguished between nature and culture which is very much prominent in the west. This is why the Indian literary field is flooded with moral stories like *Rishi Valmiki (Valmiki the Saint)* or the stories in *Panchatantra* where the animals are personified and embossed with human communicative values and are manifested with high and low moral values – an ironic representation of the human society characterized with endless intrigues and diplomacies. In a very similar fashion though in a different context altogether, famous Oriya writer Manoj Das records in his short story *AbolKara – Kahani* the natural essence of freedom manifested within the folk cults which where disembellished since the colonial saga began in India.

Abola takes the shape of an orphaned character whose orphanage is being celebrated as liberty from the modern social constrains within which the tradition suffers. Since he is an orphan he doesn't suffer from any versions of genealogical problems and he enjoys his freedom to the fullest. One day he meets a traveler Sanath who is on a pilgrimage along with a helper. He agrees to take Abola along with him on the pilgrimage on the condition that he will continue to tell him stories with a moral until and unless they reach their destination. But in the present social context, in the age of massive technological innovations where the entire globe can be compressed within the mini screens of mobile phones and laptops oral tales or the tales which violate the textual norms are considered as illogical and sabbatical for the society.

Before we analyze the various possibilities and the options which can be implemented and practiced across the nation and in different corners of the world it is very crucial for us to analyze the making India from Bharat. Yes the above sentence might sound a bit awkward when I am differentiating the nation 'India' from the nation 'Bharat' as semiotically the these are represented as mere language differences but beneath the linguistic hides the ideological and epistemological constructs which has perennially distorted and tarnished the rich traditional image with the western episteme which flowed in unobstructed. Bharat refers to the ancient India the traditional India or what the modern economists term in a much degraded tone as 'rural' India.

India as a nation is not a concrete jungle of skyscrapers, beautifully embellished roads and flyovers or may be different institutions strictly taking care that the discourse of modernization remains unchallenged and widely practiced. I am not denying these as anti-modern objects. My problem is not with their persistence but situation becomes coagulated when these forces start establishing their proprietorship over a multifaceted society whose unified coexistence is celebrated through differences. Bharat can be interpreted as a land of the fat bellied, brown skinned, uncivilized snake charmers and seductresses but in reality it has been one of the ancient places in the world with the most unique cultures and traditions that are still being followed in the postmodern context. Development and modernization has never been a natural process rather it has been a continuous process of colonial seduction and imposition in which the natives along the side of their colonizers took strong initiatives to transform the nation. The process of colonization was undertaken as a missionary zeal which was not a mere psychological transformation but ideological hypnotization ensnaring the Indians in their open-minded preaching.

In the essay *Coloniality and Modernity/Rationality* by Peruvian sociologist and humanist thinker Anibal Quijano, he opines:

> "In the beginning colonialism was a method of systematic repression, not only of the specific ideas, images, symbols or knowledge that were not useful to global colonial domination while at the same time the colonizers where expropriating from the colonizers there knowledge specially in mining, agriculture, engineering, as well as their products of work. The repression fell above all over the modes of knowing, over producing knowledge, of producing perspectives, of images or systems of images, symbols, modes of signification, over the resources, patterns, source of formalized and objectivized expression, intellectual or visual…The colonizers also imposed a mystified image of their own patterns, of producing knowledge and meaning… (Initially) the European culture was made seductive, (then) it gave access to power."

(Quijano ,Pg-3)

The above mentioned quotation makes it clear how colonialism was wielded across different parts of the world. Though its intensity of imposition varied from one place to another but the process remained unchanged. Though Quijano's expression and analysis where in reference with the colonial and postcolonial condition of South America but India also underwent this very severe process in the process of transforming itself into the nation India. Bharat was the nation in which every religious groups existed in complete harmony and it is this harmony which was first disrupted by the colonizers through promises and assurance that were unknown to the Indians previously. The Britishers very well understood that the majority of the residents in India are Hindus and the biggest folly that exist within the Hindu socio-cultural system was the silencing the lower class voices by the religious treachery of the upper caste.

Besides these intra-religious tensions the lower class Hindus where also pegged with innumerable limitations about their public interaction, activities and movements. On the other side the gender issues where equally severe with women being enforced to remain behind the curtains, exclusively involve themselves in the household duties and are obedient to their household masters that is their respective husbands and to the other male members. Thus the simplicity of the Christian preaching appeared to be a promising medium through which the women can escape from the suffocating patriarchal idolatry. Gradually the religious teachings along with the introduction of new literary forms and names in well articulated languages grabbed the psyche of the upper class money minded Indians who strongly supported the propagation of English education ahead of teachings in the native language. The new literary imports of the English narratives played a decisive role towards shaping the epistemological structure of modern India where the nation no more takes pride in its indigenous cults and languages rather proudly embrace an alien language and most importantly its languaging techniques towards global establishment and modernization.

Maturana referred that Languaging is indeed a major technique in which the epistemic system functions. It is not only the linguistic characteristics of the language that reins but the mode of execution is what matters. The different fashions, emotions, techniques and stylistics that are involved in its usage plays the central role. In order to delink the episteme it is important submerge the neo-colonial nation India to re-structure the indigenous nation which exists in the most balanced way of blending both the indigenous and the modern techniques so that we are no more stacked in the perverse atrocities of western modernity. Swami Vivekananda rightly said, 'We are what our thoughts have made us; so take care about what you think. Words are secondary. Thoughts live; they travel far.' It is time to unlearn our thoughts that have been imposed upon us without questioning and realize and relearn the thoughts which we should imbibe and embrace towards reaching our goal through the option of de-colonial pluriversality.

According to eminent scholar Jaideep A. Prabhu in his seminal essay *Theory and Philosophy* defines the term 'nation' in the following way:

"Indeed, while the meaning of nation has been hotly contested in academic debates on the nature of nationalism, it seems possible to discern three trends. The first is characterized not by a consensus on what constitutes the nation but by the agreement that such a thing exists extra-referentially and whose antecedents can be located in past social and cultural groupings…Scholars of the second trend…define it as a distinctively modern development that could only have emerged as a corollary of industrialization and the emergence of large-scale capitalism. Finally, adherents of the third trend…argue that the nation is not a subject or object but a set of relationships and thus constitutes a dynamic network cluster in which power is created and through which it is channelled."

(Prabhu, *Theory and Philosophy*)

The magnanimous canvas of theory and philosophy has performed excruciatingly from time to time to solve or evacuate innumerable intellectual confusions. Quite unfortunately, it has figured a receding enigma while addressing issues of nation and nationality. The situation appears to be more complicated in the east or to be more precise within the premises of India. The problem which has been perennially inflicting the 'Third World' nations is not only the haunting of the colonial shadows but also to conjoin the dissected and the deflected parts of the nation which were ripped apart by the colonizers. Due to multiple versions of colonial and postcolonial exploitations nations like India have ramified into uncountable socio-cultural and political branches but their visionless approach has utterly impinged them.

These above mentioned colonial tensions which have smoothly transgressed into the post-colonial generation after India's independence have inflicted a deep impact over influencing the present epistemic structure which is a highly confusing. After Independence liberty created a massive ideological void which became impossible for the natives to fill up. This ideological void was created already during the colonial era through continuous repression and paralyzing the native thought process which lost all its capability to think in its own indigenous way.

Walter Mignolo in his essay *De-linking* highlights that in the era of media and communication modernity and modernization are being sold as a 'package trip to the promise land of happiness' (3) When people show an aversion towards the accepting these norms against their own tradition the result is the infliction of 'violence' which is manufactured both physically and epistemologically. The rhetoric that naturalizes the thought process of 'modernity' also hides on its darker side the influencing cults of 'coloniality.' In order to destabilize the 'perverse logic' as Fanon points out, underlying the quandaries of the socio-political complicacies should be effaced through 'decolonizing the mind' (Thiongo) and 'imaginary' (Gruzinski) – that is 'knowledge' and 'being.'

Immediately after independence India got involved in deciding the ideological center in the field of politics and it gave rise to cheap sentimentalism and extreme propagandism. On one side when Pandit Nehru is devotedly engaged in assuring economic advancement of the nation, the Marxist admirers are busy in framing and de-framing political movements in different rural areas of the nation with the assistance of the newly evolved Indian middle class. India has always lurched in utter dilemma while constructing a definite political ideology.

The global execution of power has been a continuous process of 'legitimizing' and de-legitimizing' various versions of thoughts and ideas through the masqueraded versions of logic and reason. In fact the global dissemination of 'logic' and 'reason' altogether needs to be questioned. The western encounter with the east is associated with a painful demystification whose canvas is filled with array of images as established through Goethe's *Mahomets gesang'* or Hugo's *Adienx de l'hotesse arabe.'* It is highly upsetting to come across characters like Sir Kenneth in Walter Scott's *The Talisman* who through fighting Sarasen in the Palestinian generalizes the western orientalist mentality. The same form of epistemic dissemination is visible in Benjamin Disraeli's *Tancred* who honors the Orient in the following words, 'An Oriental lives in the Orient, he lives a live of Oriental ease, in a state of oriental despotism and sensuality, imbued with a feeling of Oriental fatalism.'

Indian nationalism and western neo- liberalism are long entangled with the debacle of coloniality hidden under the rhetoric of modernity. But it is highly needful to explore the possibilities of both the Indian thinkers and the westerners to think and act together to expel the western liberalists from intervening of what is best for the post-partition independent India rather than letting the natives do so. Science and Technology which has been the most promising weapon in the arsenal of western ideology is both imperial and liberating. Rather to be more apt, I think the liberating notion of the western science creates the illusion of freedom in order to masquerade its imperial designs which is unleashed upon the globe through the ideologues of capitalism and warfare. Understanding of the knowledge and being, should be preferred over science, western epistemology should be diminished and the approach should be made more meticulous and subjective through a well defined gnoseological approach. This will surely help us to proceed towards our dream of critical cosmopolitanism within which pluriversality will be the universal project towards emancipating our desired de-colonial goal. Walter Mignolo in his seminal essay *Prophets Facing Otherwise: The Geopolitics of*

Knowledge and Colonial Difference boldly declares, 'Therefore what seems progressive within the local history of the modern west turns out to be straightforwardly conservative in the traditional east or the non-west' (112, *Social Epistemology*). It has been enough that the river of episteme has flowed from the west to the rest. We are all standing in the most crucial juncture in which we should disentangle ourselves from shackles of coloniality or neo-colonialism by silencing the western ideology towards description and museumification of the east and forcing the west to listen to the eastern voice.

Vivekananda through his *Advaita* philosophy and Bahá'u'lláh in his Bahaistic faiths have chiseled highly flourishing existential policies which can confidently debate and over-power the Eurocentric concepts of Heidegger, Marcel, Foucault or Lacan. The essence and the existence of religion has to be deeply ensured within the highly inflative principles of moral education that the educational institutions profligate.

Both divinely and linguistically we have thoroughly observed that few words associ-ated with 'mother' or 'love' can be easily expressed in both oral and actions. Language has long been de-structured from the Saussurean etymology and re-defined in terms of human attitude and behavior. Even in the field of performing and visual arts 'Silence' has been ap-prehended as a very promising mode of communication. Even *Bhagavad Gita* consists of ample of instances of rationally upholding the principles of existence through the values of Karma Yoga. The text appeases innumerable unattended questions which even the highly acclaimed philosophers also failed or simply excused it as a mere existential or absurd phe-nomenon. According to the Gita Yoga teaches us the art to promote positive and successfully completed actions. According to the 3rd Chapter of *Brihadaranyaka Upanishad,* 'A man be-comes good by good action and bad by bad action.' The saying can be easily aligned with the Newton's Third Law of Gravity which says, 'To every action there is an equal and opposite reaction.' The law of Karma fights every form of chaos and fatalism.

Now when we are speaking of Karma it is important to control our width of thoughts and steeply concentrate on our daily actions of our life. If we supervise the pathetic condition of the nation we will successfully realize that it is because of our constant declination in our thoughts and actions that have procured such a result. Behind the development of the nation no policies or philosophies can cultivate magic plants to ensure transformations overnight. No 'Make in India' or 'Rurban' policies can convert the long cherished dreams into reality. It is the lack of self-realization that has always starved the growth of individual and the society.

We have all fallen into the cauldron which we have partly retained from our lack-lustrous traditions and partly we have borrowed from our colonizers. It is the basic teachings of the Vedanta that can always help us before we surrender ourselves to tremendous depression and realize that 'our chains of habit are too weak to be felt till they are too strong to be broken' (Samuel Johnson).

It was far ahead of the discovery of the so many theories that Swamiji had already architectured the blueprint for a well balanced rational development of the nation India. We all remember that the undivided nation was termed as Bharat, before it fell into the torturous hands of the colonizers and later on it got intertwined into the net of corruption. But ignoring his valuable teachings we all fell a victim to utter objectification, materialization and commercialization which has transformed us from simple human beings into intellectual robots. We are all enslaved by the 'virtues' of currencies which evokes a never satiating lust for wealth. Reputed philosopher T.S. Thomas has rightly said in his work *Images of Man: A Philosophic and Scientific Inquiry* that, 'Twentieth century neurosis is the neurosis of purposelessness, valuelessness, hollowness and emptiness' (1974). With the advent of the modern era, the world suddenly subtly revised itself from a hardcore theocentric world to a homocentric world. But as time matured, we have all been imprisoned into the cocoon of logocentrism. It is the *Logos* or the word which rules the roost. Eminent post-colonial novelist and critic also expressed his fear towards the power of the word which was defined in more creative and broader perspective under the term 'discourse.'

The aspect of culture and civilization has always procured a complicated field of debate in our discourse. The definition of culture or more aptly national culture has varied amongst scholars from different fields. Frantz Fanon described national culture in his essay 'On National Culture' as:

> "A national culture is not a folklore, not an abstract populism that believes it can discover the people's true nature. It is not made up of the inert dregs of gratuitous actions, that is to say actions which are less and less attached to the ever-present reality of the people. A national culture is the whole body of efforts made by a people in the sphere of thought to describe, justify, and praise the action through which that people has created itself and keeps itself in existence."

(Frantz Fanon, *The Wretched of the Earth,* 233)

In a very similar fashion the scientists, anthropologists or the archaeologists have defined and debated the term culture in different ways, none of them could produce any fruitful and sonorous results. The complicated array of words, might have intellectually honed the individual skills, may have fetched them innumerable awards and honors but in reality it has always painted a null and void picture. Even the popular dictionaries never provide a true and satisfying definition of culture. The 'hollowness' and the 'emptiness' pointed out by Thomas has finally got expressed in the tiring words of G.K. Chesterton, 'When you don't have something to believe in, you believe in everything.' This half hearted character of the human civilization protrudes with the 'causeway chill' (*The Scholar Gypsy*, Mathew Arnold) that has infiltrated and exploited our soul, burning us into dried skeletons lying in the midst of dull, barren 'Wasteland' (T.S.Eliot). The voracious inflow of material culture have displaced and gobbled all forms of spiritual values and reforms. The spirit has to be strongly guarded against the devilish powers of endless avarice.

We are no longer eager to loiter along the peripheries and borders of epistemic involvements rather it is time to disrupt the entire structure that creates these distinctions. We are no more interested in adhering with the western epiphanies how 'Who are we?' It is time for us to address this question in the de-colonial perspective so that it is with the assistance of divine traditional roots we can harness a re-contextualized form of divine-modern epistemic system which will enable us to create an indigenous identity within the vast global framework which will surely enable us to 'image a future outside colonial crisis and postcolonial failure' (Simon Gikandi, *Decolonization and Utopia*).

Works Cited

Sanskrit Shloka. Web. 2010. <http://www.sanskrit.us/vidya.htm>

Foucault, Michel. *Discipline and Punish: The Birth of Prison.* Trans. Alan Sheridan. New York: Pantheon Books, 1977. Print.

Said, Edward. *Orientalism.* New York: Vintage Books, 1978. Print.

Scott, Walter. *Talisman.* BiblioLife, 2008. Print.

Disraeli, Benjamin. *Tancred: Or, the New Crusade.* Andesite Press, 2015. Print.

Quijano, Anibal. *Coloniality and Modernity/Rationality* Cultural Studies, 21:2, 168-178. Web. 2007. <http://dx.doi.org/10.1080/09502380601164353>

Escobar, Arturo. *Worlds and Knowledges Otherwise.* Cultural Studies, 21:2, 179-210. Web. 2007. Print.

Mignolo, Walter D. *Delinking.* Cultural Studies, 21:2, 449-514, 2007. Print.

Mignolo, Walter D. *Prophets Facing Sidewise.* Social Epistemology, 19:1, 111-127, 2005. Print

Gikandi, Simon. "Decolonization and Utopia." EFL University, Shillong Campus. 3rd July.2015. Lecture.

Fanon, Frantz. *The Wretched of the Earth.* Trans. Constance Farrington. New York: Grove Press, 1963. Print.

Prabhu, Jaideep A. *Theory and Philosophy.* Web.2015. <http://jaideepprabhu.org/category/>

Maturana, Humberto R. The *Tree of Knowledge: The Biological Roots of Human Understanding.* Shambhala Publishers, 1992. Print.

Das, Manoj. *Abolkara Kahani.* Odisha: Granth Mandir, 2002. Print.

Bhabha, Homi. 'Of Mimicry and Man: The Ambivalence of Colonial Discourse' in *The Location of Culture,* 85-92, Web.1994. <http://prelectur.stanford.edu/lecturers/bhabha/html>

Rethinking Contemporaneity: Ushering a Neo-dynamic Society

The global dissemination of the concept of contemporaneity, within the matrixes of multifarious modernity programs by negating the preternatural 'cosmos' and the geo-political 'nomos,' ignites unresolved debates questioning the very justified implication of the term. The postmodern philosophers researching on de-coloniality/de-colonialism have already asserted the concept of modernity as a simulated version of coloniality or colonialism. Modernity is nothing more than a simulacrum of reality in which a abstract sheen of deception is continuously conceptualized, created and executed for seducing individuals towards an illusionary world of dreams and liberty where the liberal perceptions of unity or diversity are being heralded within a totalitarian allegory where every forms of individual uniqueness is being evacuated in the name of globalization. The concept of contemporaneity or contemporariness is vast and ambivalent as it varies within the respective junctures of time and space. But the current fashion of totalitarianism has consistently erased these junctures in order to propagate its own hegemonic discourse. Usually the multidimensional perspectives of contemporaneity are being presented in a mere objective-capitalist state but initially its functioning commences from the semantic-pragmatic point of view. Arjun Appadurai in his essay *Disjuncture and Difference in the Global Cultural Economy* analyzes that:

> "…the political narratives that govern communication between elites and followings in different parts
> of the world involve problems of both a semantic and pragmatic nature…audiences may be subject to
> very different sets of contextual conventions that mediate their translation into public politics."
>
> (Appadurai: 1990, p. 300)

The contemporariness functions according to the power of words and also the various individual and institutional processes involved towards the execution of these words. The inception of the various post-modern functionalities seems to be a mere imitation of Plato's 'Cave Allegories' where the truth is perceived in its shadows. Plato defies the Aristotelian perceptions of constructivism which believes in systematic controlling, where unidirectional thoughts are being legitimized and then propagated amongst the masses through the weapons of knowledge which leads to categorization and classification. Through this process of classification the hegemonic system builds up to marginalize a major section of the society, negating their past, constructing version of (hyper) reality where the borderline between the 'real' and 'virtual' fades away into total oblivion. The present in which we all live in is not a self realized version but form articulated through mere seduction and then we are all thrown into a huge cauldron of *jouissance* (pleasure) where everything exists in a highly contradictory, intermingled state.

The gaze of globalization have always been towards a highly privileged minority where everything appears to be utopic and well furnished which actually disrupts and divulges our attention from the non-privileged or the negated ones. The concept of contemporariness has nothing been more than a process of promoting one side of the globe that actually satisfies all the norms and conditions of commercialism and rejects the other side. In the post-Aristotle or post-Plato era, the intellectual firmament underwent major shifts in its thoughts and actions. Theories and philosophies flooded the knowledge field. It was during this time when the various disciplines deliberately violated their limited contours to invade the other disciplines resulting towards inter-disciplinarian and trans-disciplinarian developments. But the very objective of theory has undergone continuous exploitations and violations over the ages.

If we see into the etymological origin of the term we find that the term 'theory' has originated from the Greek word *theoros* which means spectator and from Latin word *theoria* which means contemplation or speculation. And what is the responsibility of a spectator? Our common sense reveals to speculate and observe the reality from different corners. But the current situation seems that Lyotard's voice have failed to flourish across and over the globe and have consistently failed to come out of the totalitarian structure or disrupt the center that continues to play the center-periphery game. Eminent postmodern philosopher Jean Francois Lyotard through his seminal essay *The Postmodern Condition* philosophized that every versions of grand/meta-narrative should be sliced into multiple versions of little narratives so that the over-arching analytical method can be dispensed at the cost of individualism. But the construct of narrative is itself a universal concept within which multiple versions of narratives engage into a never ending tussle of occupying the center and own the privilege of wielding power. The concept of an ideal world was long time back given by Thomas More in his eminent work *Utopia* which has always been both an epistemic and a symbolic referent over ages. But Utopia itself ignites multiple controversies while addressing the issues in a very self-contradictory style.

The deceptions of contemporariness are very much prominent in the text, as the various terms and conditions create geo-political controversies at several levels. The very shape of the island, representing a crescent moon is thick at the centre and narrow towards its edges.

The very concept of equalization and systematization towards articulating a perfect nation-state never blooms successfully because in the current perspective it was nothing more than what Appadurai claims as 'Indianization for Sri Lankans, Vietnamization for the Cambodians, Russianization for the people of Soviet Armenia and Baltic Republics (1990:300).' Usually whenever the term globalization is enunciated within discussions or debates it is the image of the west that psychologically invades our mind. The west can be dissected into two broad sections the one that existed before Second World War and the one that exists after it.

Utopia is the product of the west that existed prior to the world wars and it is this global minority which has designed its own colonial programs. If we have to intervene into the current fashion of contemporaneity we have to meticulously analyze how one continent waved its entire control over the globe and there comes the issue of modernity/coloniality research programs. According to me, modernity is a legitimizing process through which pseudo-structures of existence are blanketed in the shroud of a virtual realism through a continuous process of expropriation and appropriation in all the fields of human epistemology. Often the post-colonial scholars nostalgically look behind towards harnessing utopian dreams of achieving perfection which masquerades the perceptions of master-slave relationships through the frequent uses of terms like 'liberty', 'equality', 'freedom' which are immediately juxtaposed with the ideologues of speaking in favor of exploitative notions that propagated colonialism in disguise.

So, as I was speaking of dissecting the west into two major sections, the West with capital 'W' flourished very much after the Renaissance during which voyages in different parts of the world was financed by the church for the invading and discovering new lands. The mission under 'modernization' undertook its flight when Germany, Spain and Portugal turned towards the Americas for the sake of exploring the nature and civilizing its natives. The discovery of the continent of Latin America instigated a new world order which never existed prior to their invasion where the invaders very soon realized the promising trading possibilities of the place which will surely benefit the European minority. The present scenario in Latin America is not much different. It is still the 'Western' European dominators and their Euro-North American descendants are still the principal beneficiaries together with the non-European part of the world.

Usually the perspective of modernization is being represented through the lens of capitalism and commercialism which have an objective representation. But the very impulse of its beginning commences through psychological manipulation and it can only commence through the system of languaging or the process of executing language. Eminent Chilean biologist Humberto Maturana in his book *The Tree of Knowledge* uses the perceptions of neurons and the human body functioning system towards the development and functioning of the epistemic system of modernity. According to Maturana the human society functions as the system of organism and its niches. The niches are the like interconnected neurons crisscrossing with each other but their joints are distinctly visible. The epistemic violence unleashed by the Europeans evacuated these distinctive spots in the name of unity in diversity and ultimately they were all framed within universal superstructures interconnecting political, social and cultural dominations. This is particularly classified as Euro-centered colonialism.

According to Peruvian socialist and human thinker Anibal Quijano in his essay *Coloniality and Modernity/Rationality*:

> "In the beginning colonialism was a product of a systematic repression, not only of the specific believes, ideas, images, symbols or knowledge that were not useful to global colonial domination, while the same time the colonizers were expropriating from the colonized their knowledge, specifically in mining, agriculture, engineering, as well as their products and work."

(Maturana: 2007, p. 169)

Usually whenever the critics and experts interpret the term colonization or the later forms of developments like coloniality or neo-colonization then the violent histories of power repressions occupies the basic objects of discussions but the process started through a systematic expropriation of the native knowledge in their respective fields and also trying to identify the various negative perspectives which the native are themselves enforced with. Thus before expropriation of the local knowledge and appropriation of the colonizers' the Europeans socio-culturally seduced the natives with their alluring agendas which provided large number of natives to come out of their cloistered cults and practices. Infact the religious groups played pivotal roles sending organizations across the globe, preaching their 'open-hearted' manifestoes to the culturally backward natives in different continents.

The colonizers imposed a mystified image of their patterns to produce and impose their own system of knowledge and discipline. In order to make it attractive and special the patterns where deliberately placed out of reach from the natives and then it was made easily available to them. This process of seduction later on was transcended towards its own commercial motives which gave birth to global capitalism within which the entire globe is pursuing. In this way Cultural Europeanization was pursued as a form of aspiration which liberated the natives from the clogged traditionalism and steered them towards a dream vision, a dream world which deliberately exhausts the borderlines and to create its own borderlines. The eastern journey of the west happened much later and it has not been so severe in the continents of Africa or Asia as compared to Latin America but their attitude remained the same. The Two world wars brought a massive transgression to the global scenario and as usual from the ideological point of view. The perceptions of colonialism started undergoing rapid transformations creating multiple patterns of illusions or what Plato terms as 'Cave Allegory.' Plato claims that we are actually never associated with the reality but always lurching in the shadow of reality which he illustrates through an instance inside the cave. Suppose an individual is sitting inside the cave and he sees the sunlight sipping through the crevices illuminating the dead darkness which is present inside and he declares, 'Wow! The sunlight is so bright and energetic.' But the question is does he sees the sunlight or the reflection of the sunlight? And if it is well analyzed the answer will obviously go in favour of the second. It is at this very point where the differences between reality and illusion exhaust in a very spontaneous and unconscious way.

The colonizers, irrespective of time and space, basically invaded the regions for the sake of trade and commercial benefits. The massive industrial upsurge in Europe was well complimented with the rise of raw materials to be consistently fed to the industries and factories for rapid supply of complete goods. In order to avoid over-exhaustion of Europe the westerners turned towards the rest of the world and besides Americas found Asia and Africa as highly voluptuous and impregnated with endless raw sources. The commercial prosperity encouraged the colonizers to induce socio-economic and political transformations and it was largely influenced by the concept of Leviathanism which already waved endless debates and controversies during the 17th century. But Thomas Hobbes, besides several other political philosophers played a crucial role towards propagating the concept globally and is still being followed in different re-contextualized forms. Thomas Hobbes who was a precursor of Social Contract Theory which was later on funneled by Jean Jacques Rousseau initiated the concepts of *summum bonum* and *summum malum*.

Summum Bonum means greatest good which according to Hobbes was impossible to achieve as every individuals have their own versions of good which persists in conflict with each other and also plays a pivotal role towards inducing warfare. The other side of it lies in *summum malum* which resorts to the greatest evil the ultimate fear of a painful death. Thus Hobbes predicts a malevolent future psycho-physically crippled:

> "In such condition there is no place for industry, because the fruit thereof is uncertain, and consequently, not culture of the earth, no navigation, nor the use of commodities that may be imported by sea, no commodious building, no instruments of moving and removing such things as require much force, no knowledge of the face of the earth, no account of time, no arts, no letters, no society, and which is worst of all, continual fear and danger of violent death, and the life of man, solitary, poor, nasty, brutish, and short."

(Hobbes)

In order to avoid such a glum future he gives the proposal of the commonwealth which is one of the key ingredients towards the modern concept of hegemony which is an integral part of neo-colonialism in the contemporary era. The implication of the term 'commonwealth' has always been self-contradictory because in order to avoid socio-political anarchy it encourages a compromise theory within which individuals should introduce self restraint by sacrificing a few of their own rights, explicitly or forcefully, to the higher institutional authority in return to seek protection for the rest of their rights. This very concept forms the roots of democracy which claims to recognize people's rights but the common mass is captured within illusionary ideologue which doesn't allow but enforce them.

In the process of legitimization and naturalization of the various prospects of contemporary existence, the individual being is continuously encrusted with existential limitations. These limitations successfully dissipate into the individual lives through collective hypnotization which creates a virtual garb of liberty within which hides the dominant antiquities commercial gains. According to Nelson Maldonado-Torres in his essay *On the Coloniality of Being: Contributions to the development of a concept* reveals that:

> "The idea was that colonial relations of power left profound marked not only in the areas of authority, sexuality, knowledge and the economy, but on the general understanding of being as well. "

(Maldonado-Torres: 2007, p. 242)

The philosophy of Descartes, 'I think, therefore I am' or Heideggerian philosophy of 'I am therefore, I think' has always nurtured the Eurocentric epistemological veins through the construction of an illusionary self which is nothing but the masqueraded image of the colonizer. Within this framework the individual undergoes a stringent form of rhizomation through continuous negation. The very declaration of 'I think' or 'I am' is a deliberate self-proclamation through which the Eurocentric self is asserted by negating the others. 'I think' ensures the others cannot think and 'I am' ensures the non-existence of other beings. The coloniality of power outlines the smooth transition of domination through exploitation and it functionabilities spreads across different areas of knowledge production.

It is this captivation of the self which finally contributes towards creating and ideological and intellectual void which is another trick of contemporaneity. Analysing in the context of a nation India, it was declared independent sixty nine years before but the concept of democracy and independence is itself under serious question because the very perspectives have been mis-interpreted and mal-practiced since the natives where won the space to be in charge of their own geo-political space. This confusion of native existence which has been deliberately created by the colonizers is what Hannah Arendt phrases as 'No Longer and not yet' in her book *Essays in Understanding 1930-1954: Formation, Exile and Totalitarianism.* She compares the generational transformation of the human civilization with the metamorphoses of silkworms to butterflies. One generation of humans passes away and is taken away by the other generation which leads to the decline of the old and the birth of the new. This continuous process is not an epicurean transformation but highly filled with disruptions which creates an empty space or a 'kind of historical no man's land.' This no man's land what Hannah Arendt terms as 'no longer and not yet.' But Arendt's analysis also fails to intervene and crack through the deception of 'no man's land' which is actually a 'selective man's land.' It is this space which the power mongers have been using perennially exploiting to dupe the masses with their futile assurances, promises through the weapons of global digitalization not enjoying the license to create a highly private platform at the cost of the public interest. Dr. Homi Bhabha, coined the term 'ambivalence' to designate current global scenario which has degraded towards a paradoxical epistemic disintegration.

Before I continue with my further discussions and analysis, I would like to elucidate that in the coming paragraphs I am going to describe the nation India in a metonymic fashion and the term contemporaneity/contemporariness will be strangulated of its totalitarian identity of being a mission and will be shattered into multiple options which can function in its own liberating ways and can successfully dissipate through every potholes of human socio-cultural existence. Contemporaneity has always functioned as a metaphor for the propagation of Eurocentrism globally. But our very approach towards the Eurocentric perspectives has always been flawed. The very hegemony of Eurocentrism has been weaved within the continent itself before being tunneled across the globe. The Europe which is being mediated and channelised all over the world is a capitalist minority within a minority. From the cartographical point of view the continent which is already a small one as compared to the global rest, is further eco-politically confined within the financial yardstick of Euros. In other words, the Europe that reigns along with United States of America is actually the economically flourishing ones and to ensure their consistent global promotions the media undertakes excruciating initiatives. Usually in the oriental side of the globe most of the newspapers engage discussions and debates regarding the western European nations financially and economically prosperous and the socio-politically tumultuous eastern Europe hardly finds a space to generate themselves or sometimes out of sympathy they are given the smallest space available. We have consistently failed to realize that there is a West within a west, an exploitative Contingent within a continent, an Occident within an occident.

Neo-colonialism/Capitalism/Contemporaneity has exhausted its fetish towards specifically distinguishing regions and has attained the role of the being the greatest opportunist and this opportunism fails to identify the individual *nomos* or specific ideological regions within a definite time and space. Eminent German Jurist and political theorist Carl Schmitt is of the notion that the first thing that modernity/comtemporaneity programs do is to violate the individualities of the beings and though usually it is physically represented, but its primary articulation starts through massive psychological annihilation. Thus capitalism is no more an all encompassing wings of the immortal Phoenix but in order to make philosophies look attractive and innovative multiple sub-layers have been generated to instigate the common mass. The multi-layered versions of theorizing and philosophizing have successfully generated a limited group of multi-dimensional truths which are dominant in its own ways. The multi-dimensional imageries generated by the truths successfully entice and hypnotizes the common mass within its dominating hermeneutics. Thus, baptizing the entire concept as Layer Theory, I further elaborate how its functionability needs to be realized towards establishing a de-colonial, de-linked version of the present which Gerhard Richter terms as *Afterness*.

Richter a German visual artist and one of the pioneers of New European Painting significantly questions the various prospects of afterness :

> "What does it really mean, for something to "follow" something else either in language or as a concept? Can the "after" ever fully emancipate itself from its predecessor or does it infact remain in the latter's ghostly and largely unacknowledged debt? The after is not merely a temporal dimension."
>
> (Richter, p. 2)

But the global capitalist designs rides over the temporal contemporaneity which is a major weapon towards prosperity. The concepts of 'before' and 'after' are ambivalent terms which is very difficult to confine within specific contours of time and space. With reference to the contemporary significance it can be broadly trisected into pre-colonial, colonial and post-colonial. Keeping aside the first category, since the very inception of the colonial stage, the perennial process of ideographic thermolysis began which has been propelled to the contemporary era as ideological epitasis. It is in this very transformation the interception and impositions of layering comes to the question. 'Before' and 'after' has hardly been a continuation for the Third World Nations but has been a highly disrupting and degenerating construct from time to time.

From Shakespeare, through Pope, across Dryden into several modern and postmodern philosophers, acceptance or rejection of the ancients has always been a spurious topic for literary debate. Since a century this debate has been expanded and transported in an inter-disciplinary mode to affect all the other possible elements of human existence. The colonising version of afterness was affiliated towards the expropriation of the native cults which where alienated into the reject of being 'before and backward' and imposing the 'modern' facets over the natives. But in order to delink or decolonize the very concept of the present which largely relies on the visionary perspectives of 'afterness' by introducing a middle path in which the past/present or before/after will persist in symbiosis with each other. Thus it is time not to replace but to displace, to negate the Eurocentric negativities, introducing the series of options through unlearning the west and relearning through border thinking. It is time to disable and dispose ideography and ideology and promote nomothetic elements which invites logic and reason through parallel modes of delinking and border thinking.

Eminent professor from Princeton University Simon Gikandi in one of his lecture sessions said that decolonization and decoloniality involves two steps:

- To know the other or more specifically the European Other
- To disengage oneself.

The primary stage to disentangle contemporaneity is to realize the differences and the similarities. Every nation in the world is blessed with different states of histories and genealogies which have been disintegrated through colonialism. But the histories, supposed of India and Africa, has always been a part of European imagination. If we steer back to the works of Herodotus and his contemporaries we find evidences of the names of India and Africa under different nomenclatures. India and Africa where never colonized in the same fashion. Thus, while working on the perspectives of decolonization, the theological structure of India can never match with the humanistic struggle in Africa and this where post-colonialism fails to function.

As we speak about decolonization or delinking of contemporariness in contemporaneity, humanism and humanistic issues automatically falls into the frontline. The question of humanities has always been a problematic one. Colonial Humanities invented the human beings as the non-humans or in other words those who didn't confirm to the Eurocentric notion of humanism. When we engage discussions about India, Africa or may be Latin America most of the times we are unaware about their originalities and continue to discuss. The Zapatistas, a revolutionary leftist political and militant group based in Chiapas, the southernmost state of Mexico declares, 'Because we are equal we have to different.' It is difference in equality and the equalities in difference which must be harnessed in order reclaim and reorder the layers of our existence or what I favour to term as the Layer Theory. The tension of ideas that exists between individuals or may be within the different consciences of the same individual is a crucial element to understand the prospects of the present. Thus in order to recreate or reform the concept of contemporaneity the journey must embark through self-assertion of the self by the self not by the other or the other of the self. To simplify, the west has been defining not only its own self but has also mysteriously taken the responsibility on its own shoulders to define the others as well or may be doing the same in a differently manipulative way.

Professor Gerald Taiaiake Alfred of Victoria University in one of his speeches about the *Mohawks* strongly voices that:

> "These are my words. These are my thoughts. I am a Mohawk person. I am come from the community of Mohawks. But here I am not representing my community but I am speaking of myself…I am not talking about the Indians. But I am talking as an Indian who belongs to the Indian community. "
>
> (Gerald Taiaiake Alfred, on the *Mowhawks*)

And yes! This is the very first step towards decolonization, asserting the self through establishing a sepulcher of oral discourse which needs to be re-enlivened and practiced. The system of oralism will not only assist towards chiseling vibrant genuine voices but will also help in the process of unraveling the multifaceted hidden layers which remains subdued under one form of totalitarianism or the other. Alfred seems to be very conscious and sensible enough while articulating his discourse where he displays a superb form of 'unity in diversity' or what the diasporic language terms as 'salad bowl.' But the contemporariness and its vast platter of socio-political designs like 'socialism', 'democracy' or 'liberty' seems to have an allergic attitude towards it. Already discussed in the earlier section of the essay that in modernity, languaging is a crucial aspect and it is upon this very prospect that democracy builds its own kingdom of exploitation. Moreover there lie obvious discrepancies between the term 'orality' and 'languaging.' From the linguistic point of view though they function in the same way but the system of languaging is a modern/colonial invention which over powers the traditional mode of speech which is denounced as oral.

History reveals that the term democracy originated in Greece, but with the passage of time it has been tampered with the concepts of modern-imperial, Euro-nation states which were purely constructed on marginalization and modern racism. The concept of democracy originally lies in its possibility. It is a process to create a space for everybody to vote, to assert their rights in the gentlest way. But the colonizers distempered it in order to give it an exploitative, seducing face which doesn't give any provisions to those ancient ideologues which propagated the best possible attitudes. In ancient China the concept of *He/Ho* (harmony), in Africa the concept of *Ubuntu* (friendly, cooperative and commercial life), in Latin America the concept of *Sumakkausag* (to live in plenitude), all alluded to the present concept of democracy which is being preached but never practiced. So we are looking forward towards not de-westernizing but de-colonizing contemporaneity as de-westernization is nothing more than a fraudulent side of neo-colonialism which physically removes itself to articulate a Foucauldian *Panopticon* which haunts or seduces the individual through their ideas.

The biggest challenge in the process of decolonization is to propagate the layer theory through disentangling every version of institutional compartmentalization which legitimizes the illegitimate and vice-versa and it happens through the usage of languages. It is time to go beyond the postmodern to be alter-modern within which the signifier and the signified no more exists so harmoniously with each other as it persisted during the Saussurean times. In the era of hyperrealism where we are all encased within the cocoon of hyperrealism the signifiers continues to remain constant but the signified makes a continuous shuffling like the rapid movement of a wide array of images. It is the shadow within which we persist. In order to further elaborate the concept of layer theory which I have already mentioned in the earlier

31

part of the essay I would like to speak about how India transformed itself from a nation into the Nation. Pre-colonial and post-colonial India intermediated by the two and the half century phase of colonization brush up significant imageries and concepts towards the formulation of the present.

Ancient Indian society as per the scriptures and the classical texts are well nurtured through certain bordering amenities – caste, class, gender, community, language and religion. The very first element is a very unique feature in India which has always socio-culturally kept the nation apart from the globe. When the colonizers or to be more specific colonizing Britishers arrived in India they as usual came with trading interests, but soon they 'realized' the divine necessity to teach and civilize the dark regions of the earth which according to them are lurching in utter darkness. The process was initiated through the religious missions, quite sensibly identified the negative prospects of the Indian religious traditions, which unlike Christianity are infested and infected with multiple caste and communal politics. This multi-layerism within every cross roads of an Indian existence indeed make it a highly excruciating task to remove the kernel, object by object, but it has to happen and it is never impossible! We should always keep in mind that like every colonial inceptions the concept of contempo-raneity has its own sub-layered versions of totalitarianism which is why the Spivackian con-cept of the subaltern cannot be placed on the same couch with Queer Theory. A Dalit woman or in a broader sense the causes of a Dalit in general cannot be addressed and nurtured within the premises of Fourth World. Moreover the very socio-political divisions of the globe – First world, Second world, Third and Fourth World are the products of the Europe rather to be more specific the minor Europe.

In order to override the west, we have to first invade them, appropriate, explore but not influenced by their unhygienic potions of influence and then expropriate the deceptive shroud of imposition which has always veiled our vision. It is nothing more than using the same weapon to disengage our mind and body. So, as I just differentiated the elements of oral cult with the contemporary concept of languaging earlier, it is very important for us to realize that our very existence undertook its legion if prosperity over and across the globe riding through oral practices. The very anthropological origin of the oral culture dates back to the time when human life evolved. There were no theoretical system of expression and institu-tional or industrial manufacturing system to generate rapid force of thoughts and ideas and the only source was the oral tongue. Through genetic and hormonal *poiesis*, human civilization continued to evolve in much advanced and better ways and in the process, much before the invention of writing, it was the individual voice, the free flowing manifestation of the self that created every ethics of our contemporary knowledge on which we are feeding.

With respect to Indian and African cult's oral forms of communication was not simply a medium of construct or expressions but also the indigenous arc through which individual voice enjoyed the provision of their respective space. Even a couple of decade back, India still enjoyed was still blessed with storytelling bards dominated the rural scene and the still the young child slept in his/her grandmother's lap through the moral thoughts as orally tunneled by her. Long before the advent of allegorical tales by the west, India's oral tales were well enriched with allegorical elements exposing or criticizing the human intrigues. The *Kavigaan* (musical poetry) folk tradition of Bengal, the masked *Yakshagana* theatrics of Karnataka or may be the tribal language of the *Jarawas* or *Onges* of Andamans all have contributed to the rich legacy of the Indian cult. The above sentence which actually appears very non-linear and non-connected deliberately brings in the expressional, linguistic and anthropological perspective onto the same platform to give a minute illustration the multidimensional aesthetics and hermeneutics involved in the formulation and establishment of the indigenous India which has long been disembellished of its own character and has been the experimental ground for contemporaneity or to be more apt neo-colonial contemporariness which we are all expressing.

May be Kavigaan, Yakshagana or the tribal languages emerge from three disjointed backgrounds but their inter-collaborative and collective diversity cannot be ignored. Especially talking about the Kabigaan folk traditions, the famous figure Hensman Anthony or better known as Anthony Firingee attained a lot of fame as a kaviyaal (the performer of the Kavigaan). He was of Portuguese origin, arrived in India as a traveler and settled in Farashdanga in the Chanderrnagar region of West Bengal. With the passage of time his interaction with the Bengal music traditions was never a matter of displacement and western monopolization but of healthy exchanges. As he entertained the natives with his Portuguese tunes on his mandolin similarly he also adapted to the then prospective tradition of Kavigaan which was an integral part of Bengali religious culture. Kavigaaa's were basically a lyrical-oral exchange amongst two groups of people lead by the *Kaviyals* or *Sarkars* (leaders). They were accompanied by the *Dohars* who often repeated behind what their leaders sang. The competitive spirit was evoked in a very divine fashion through offering musical allusions to the Goddess

Ganesha or Saraswati. The Kavigaan was divided into four parts – *sakhi-samvad, biraha, lahar and kheur*. Each of these aspects of the song are encrusted with separate emotions which are being expressed and exchanged in the form of questions and answers or *sawal-jawab* which is a very crucial part if Indian art and aesthetics.

Besides these the several folk versions that formed the very basis of the Indian theatrics, have been substantiated and awarded a distressed identity which doesn't fit within the nation India. *Jatras* in Bengal, *Nautanki* in Uttar Pradesh and Bihar or the *Bhavai* in Gujarat are nomeclatured within the singular terminology of swangs which always possess negative complementation. These have failed to be a part of the famous pop culture and have been tagged as a degraded, barbaric version of the high aesthetics being practiced and nurtured by the uncivilized rustic folk. Isn't this attitude a slant reflection of the very British notions imposed upon the nation? The very first question that arises is how we can define India as a Nation or place her within the perceptions of a postmodern totalitarian state when we have so many tiny nations hidden within. India's oral traditions have not only been a fascination within but also out and moreover oral exchanges seemed to be more powerful and rapid for inter-cultural and intra-cultural exchanges as compared to the contemporary instruments of technocracy. Technological gadgets have longtime back moved beyond its basic functions to allure the global mass with its 'extra' facilities which encourages the people to engage within multiple functioning within a single gadget. The modern language of contemporaneity rests on technological benefits which create an entirely new world of ethics which uphold a very organized and disciplined form of existence and the very first thing it does in the process is negating all the natural and traditional aspects of a nation.

The very first step to reject is through de-legitimizing the internal and asserting the immoral, illogical external which contributes towards the very construct of the present. With the independence of the nation the conch of modernizing the nation in order to upbring it to the global level was blown. The very concept of modernity that was harnessed by the newly appointed government didn't confirm with most of the cults of the pre-colonial India which were already confiscated and dumped by the Britishers. The very framework of the Indian constitution bore signs of coloniality through its borrowings from the various western constitutional features. It does sound a bit weird, but the very Indianness of the Indian constitution comes into the question. If the constitution comprises of even the best parts of the different world bodies, it is nothing more than a mere emblem of the colonizing west. The ideological, psychological and the geo-political gap that was generated by the britishers where filled once again with the very elements of coloniality. Nation, nationalism and nationhood were defined within the heteronormative perspectives which are nothing more than exploitative designs to fill their personal coffers.

The very birth of modernity took place in India through the hands of the elite class gentry who where nothing more than the mere puppets in the hands of the colonizers. Allured by some worthless, futile 'awards' as given by the colonizers in the forms of titles or small land grants they enthusiastically remained the 'noble savage' to the colonizers. In order to bring a entire nation under control, the Britishers very well identified the loopholes through which they can perform. Besides the religious influences through the Christian organizations the colonizers seduced and manipulated the monarchy and the feudal lords who sat in the zenith of the Indian power prior to their arrival. With the advent of the colonizers, it was a matter of both triumph and lamentation for the natives. The colonial exploitations that the organizational historical narratives provide are nothing but just a small side of the true story. The process of colonization was both domination and seduction. In the era of theo-centrism the colonizers very well analyzed the east, understanding that for nurturing long time strategies they require the cooperation of the natives. Native cooperation meant to influence the individuals to admit such dividends which will be absolutely beneficial for their respective sense but highly detrimental for their collectivity. The religious and communal diversities already pegged with countless major and minor divisions made things very easier for the Britishers not only to influence the natives but at the same time influence conversions. Before socio-economic or political forms of colonialism, it was the religious versions of colonialism which was primarily propagated all over the nation. Though it attained a much critical identity in Africa through massive tribal conversions, but in India it was no less.

The religious transformations through getting affiliated with Catholic thoughts, was an optimistic source of liberation for the people especially the lower class Hindus or the tribals of the northern and the north-eastern part of India. This is why even when Indians visit the north-eastern part of the nation they are often welcomed with abuses like *khadaar* (outsider) which very much highlight the prevalent anti-Indian feeling in them. It was the very colonial version of religious conversions that is being re-invigorated through the present anti-secular policy of *Ghar-Wapsi* (religious conversions being practiced amongst Hindus). Christianity easily understood that it existed far beyond the entanglements of caste and community and as a result it could easily channelize its alluring policies amongst the common mass. Moreover the tribals and the lower class communities where already pestered with the monarchial regime of the different native kingdoms further worsened with the emergence of the new landed gentry a by-product of the monarchy itself. Religious exploitations where not their sole complain, but in a traditional society which maintained faith on the law books of *Manu* (Indian law maker) ahead of modern innovativeness and constructivism. If the west have sarcastically expressed India once as the land of snake-charmers and orthodoxy then they were never wrong. It might hurt our socio-cultural or religious sentiments, but in an outright way this is what India was prior to the arrival fo the colonizers.

But the very same form of modern representation is no more acceptable. Within the massive jargon of technocratic capitalism of which the entire seems to be addicted off, the eternal conscious or may be the unconscious seems to somewhere or other echo the pedagogical lamentation of Leanne Simpson, 'No one ever asked me what I was interested, nor did they ask me for my consent to participate in their system. (Simpson: 2014, p. 6). The lamentation of Simpson in her essay *Land as Pedagogy: Nishnaabeg Intelligence and Rebellious Transformation* pre-resonated during the pre-colonial to the colonial times and continues to do so in contemporary India. The very opposite extreme of constricted traditionalism was anarchism or to be more apt ideological vagabondism. The Britishers liberated the Indians from themselves to be trapped with the deceptive gyre of colonialism and to make things attractive for them, the primary medium of accessibilities were kept far out of the native reach. The parallel attraction and segregation of the native was an element of both success and humour for the colonizers because they could attract a majority of their herds into their shoes. They could very well understood that the lower class Hindus, the Muslims along with the women in common are absolutely dejected with the multi-layered system of habitual oppression within and outside the domestic boundaries.

We are already intimate with the instances of the so called outcastes like the sweepers, washer-men or the prostitutes where not allowed to access the common village well which where accessed by the *Brahmins*, *Kshatriyas* or the landlords. As a result people mistakenly accessing those or may be deliberately under severe scarcity where subjected to severe humiliations and often the women ending being sexually harassed. It is the same religious leaders who preached high morals in the temples during the day and engaged in raucous immoralities at night and the lineage continues. In modern India, religion has taken a worse direction with the cult of self-declared demi-gods feasting on the materialistic dona-tions of the common mass. Nothing just another highly aesthetic side of contemporaniety indeed! It is this version of contemporaneity where financially privileged individuals take advantages of the immoral laxities of the common mass; dupe them within their hyper-realistic constructs masqueraded within their highly purified loins of saffronization. The pro-cess started during the pre-colonial times and it still continues in a more alarming stature. Moreover the element of 'saffronization' which was earlier concocted within the preferablity of the Hindu religion has become an all encompassing political entourage in the current polit-ical context. The pre-conscious or the unconscious which exists embedded within the human psyche plays a highly motivating role towards influencing the human society with their ac-tions.

The very production of the oral thoughts which ultimately culminates into variegated actions is nothing but multiple products of the human preconscious and his/her unconscious. Human performatives in daily life depends on these deeper layers of the mind rather than the surface consciousness. During the colonial times it is this very layer that was being invaded and infected by the colonisers. In the perspective of economy, the outsiders knew very well how to control the common mass agitations which became very frequent towards the end of their rule. The resources of Indian mass movements where obviously the elite class people who where monetarily enslaved by the Britishers and which widely affected the Indian strug-gle for freedom as well. The trisected socio-political division of the nation – India, Pakistan and Bangladesh along with continuous misrepresentations through the literary texts and trans-lations kept India lurching under their shadows. The main issue that India faced was that na-tion was left in a total lack-lustrous state lurching in utter psychological void. During the pre-colonial or the colonial times the mental faculty was absolutely crippled and numbed. The sudden withdrawal of the colonial rule was an-other colonial design to operate back from their land, their own continent. If colonialism have dominated and exploited the nation the coloniality has trafficked India to the west.

The process is still continuing only in different ways and forms with the west having being expanded beyond the Eurocentric to the United States, the Freudian precon-scious/unconscious continues to hold the power within which the Althuserrian apparatuses (Ideal State Apparatus and Repressive State Apparatus) continues to function. The idealism that is being preached by contemporaneity continues to function within the grips of coloniality in different shapes. The Arab Spring Revolution, war against military dictatorships in parts of Africa or the communal wars waged by Boko Haram or ISIS only represents a mad rush after totalitarian politics and it is at this place where the surface layer has long being vanquished to reveal the multi-layered conflicts which has made the total game of contemporaneity a riddling one. When all the layers of the human being, engages into never ending tussles it is the 'Big Brother' who have the final laugh, the capitalist panopticon that keeps on eyeing upon us. When a nation is wrecked by the any forms of communal violence or terrorist attacks an array of major government officials comes up to express their concerns and grievances for the losses but later investigations which often mysteriously fades away reveals major institutional supports from the very same source. This is the very corruptive image of the present which universally persists in the present. In the present governmental scenario, innumerable policies have been formulated towards re-establishing the indigenous perspectives but it is nothing more than a mere continuation of universalism.

The "Make in India,' campaigns or the model villages which has won a lot of global recognition as highly impactful national policies are nothing but superficial efforts towards building a nation which drowns further into the vast ocean of already prevalent extreme commercialism. The theoretical functions in chiseling out the contemporaneity have to be de-shackled from colonial influences. So Leanne Simpson quite appropriately says:

> "...Theory isn't just for academics; it's for everyone...Theory...within this context is generated from the ground up and its power stems from its living resonance within individuals and collectives."
> (Simpson: 2014, p. 8)

Simpson's 'within this context' varies from one corner of the globe to another affecting the different layers and sub-layers of human existence but the pluriversal convictions against the present representation remains intact. It is time for us to think from the borders, to legitimize those ideologues which have been shoved off into the 'non' category of prefixes and always to be within the structure but never to operate from the centre. In a nutshell, it is time for us to shape multiple versions of alternate realities which will help us to propel from the east to west. The Layer Theory may appear in many cases quite absurd for the critics based on the issue if it is ever possible to reach the very core of the global problematic through continuous process of unearthing? And yes I strongly feel it is possible indeed. While dealing with the issues of de-colonialism or de-coloniality, that it is an option which supersedes every categories of time and space which are imposed through organizational missions wholeheartedly funded through specific, propagandist interests. This situation first has to be evaded and then negated from the very discourse of the human existence.

De-coloniality is a process which has to continuously nurtured and practiced by individual through the consistent process of border thinking, border epistemology and pluritopic hermeneutics. The process of unearthing the layers which I have mentioned earlier should initiate through the process of epistemic disengagement which. To simplify further, The Freudian preconscious and unconscious the two most empowering forces functioning towards shaping our consciousness should be de-toxicated of different versions of colonial or neo-colonial senses of modernity/rationality and contemporaneity. The perennially negated elements have to be restored; it is time to look beyond and behind the mirror as globalization has converted it to an object of deception. How will the child assert his/her genuine self during the Lacanian 'Mirror Stage' when the self is no more realized by the self but influenced and imposed by the other through an ideological puddle of negations and de-legitimizations of the legitimate? Border thinking enables us to look beyond the pre-notioned screen to extract and re-establish the things that has been left ignored within the westernized formats of reason and logic. It is time to define my-self through myself and not by the western outsiders and the primary step which we should all inherit is to incorporate Chicana cultural theorists Gloria Anzaldua's metaphor of border into the domain of contemporaneity.

We have to ensure that the process is more of disenfranchisement rather than disengaging. The process of disengaging might throw us outside the structure but which aggravate the causes. We have to realize our functions both within and without the system. We have to both inside and outside, so that the neo-colonial framework can be challenged and shattered from within, through pouring in the very thoughts and ideas which were discarded long time back. It is time to move beyond our clichéd forms of contemporaneity towards alter-contemporariness. But this altering will no more be a continuation of the moderni-ty/coloniality research program but de-centering the present from its usual Eurocentrism and its own linear branch of knowledge production which links Greece, Rome, Christianity and Modern Europe. Nomos needs to be restored once again which will generate a new spatio-temporal tone of modernity while disinheriting the ongoing one. The other sides of the hy-phen and the slashes should be brought into consideration so the European 'myth of moderni-ty' could be re-mythified and the focus could be drawn towards peripheralization. The peripheries needs to be restored along the centre (but not within) so that it can function independently without creating the hegemony.

As the functioning commences from the self, it is important not to decolonize the being but to decolonize our preconscious or the subconscious. This very process of delinking has to start with self-realization and self-assertion through the self and not the other. According to eminent semiotician Dr. Walter D. Mignolo, in his essay *Delinking: The rhetoric of modernity, the logic of coloniality and the grammar of de-coloniality* says:

> "Under the spell of neo-liberalism and the magic of media promoting it, modernity and modernization, together with democracy, are being sold as packaged trip to the promised land of happiness..."

(Mignolo: 2007, p. 450)

It is from this continuous process of packaging and promising we have to separate ourselves, so that the 'perverse logic' as was illustrated by Fanon in is essay *The Wretched of the Earth* no more entices us in its cobwebs. One of the biggest issues that contemporaneity faces is, unlike the ancients, they no more exclude or occlude other forms of totalities, but asserts them so that they continue to function like the androids of the present generation. In the non-European imperial language and epistemologies (Mandarin, Arabic, Bengali, Russian, Aymara, etc) the notion of totality doesn't exist and is absolutely unthinkable for them. The multiple versions not only require being unearthed but also at the same time the negated versions have to be asserted. The western epistemic norms of which shifted from theo-centrism towards ego-centrism which confirmed to the heteronormative norms highlighted the colonized vision of the being. Thus the nonwestern versions of totality have to confront with the broad imperial versions of totality.

But the issue in the present era is when the nonwestern totalities are creating their own versions of imperialism/neo-colonialism and this where the Layer Theory comes into foreplay. The multiple versions of totalities which have already generated itself through society, economy, religion and politics needs to be further sliced and excavated so that all forms of totalities cease to exist through equal exposure and functioning. Moving beyond the socio-economic policies of Marxism, Capitalism or Secularism it is time for rhetorical and hermeneutical archaeology which will continue with the excavations until and unless the bottom line is touched. The concept can b simply associated with the process of digging the ground with a shovel. Deeper the ground is dug, all the eternal elements that are present get the scope of coming out and getting scattered here and there which gives them the scope to come out and occupy a new space in the already existing ground which earlier was covered with a limited number of surface elements. Our contemporariness needs to be constructed in the same way through propagating neo-humanism of moral self-consciousness.

The upholders of self-consciousness and fellow feelings, especially a figure like Mahatma Gandhi who was a source of high motivation for formulating multiple indigenous strategies like Khadi Movement, Quit India Movement, Non-Violent Satyagraha and several others himself was a racist in his heart while being a youngster in South Africa. After being abused as a 'coolie' and being thrown out by a white man from the first-class train compartment at Pietermaritzburg on 7th Jun, 1893, he wrote an 'Open Letter' to the Natal Parliament on December 19, 1893:

> "I venture to point out that both the English and the Indians spring from a common stock, called the Indo-Aryan…This believes serves as the basis of operations of those who are trying to unify the hearts of the two races…a general believe seems to prevail in the colony that the Indians are a little better, if at all than the savages or the Natives of Africa. The Indians were, and are, in no way inferior to their Anglo-Saxon brethren, if I may venture to use the word, in the various departments of life – industrial, intellectual, political, etc…"

(Gandhi, 'Open Letter' to the Natal Parliament on December 19, 1893)

On what basis can the Indians be aligned to the 'Anglo-Saxon brethrens?' Genetically or ideologically it doesn't make any sense. But it is the same Gandhi who later on returns to India transforms himself from man of sophistication into a saintly figure. If the injection of the Euro-centric thoughts where the first form of totalitarianism, then the interjection of such anti-nationalistic thinking has led to other forms of exploitations which continue to happen today under the canopy of different party manifestoes but the cause and result is the same. But it is the same who lead his life setting examples not only for the nation but also for the entire globe as well. In the *Selected Writings of Mahatma Gandhi* Ronald Duncan describes how the Gandhi inherited the divine ethics along with modern conformations towards framing a balanced nation, an ideal nation for all the developing countries. Though it didn't happen, but the process of successfully initiated and proved to be highly influencing for the common mass. The rural folks who accounted to a major part India continuously failed to realize the necessity of hygiene in life and as a result despite several efforts they continued to relieve themselves in the open. Gandhiji never became agitated rather he himself cleaned their bowels by digging holes in the ground and burying them. After seeing their great leader doing such a humble job, they realized and joined him. This single instance can be epitomized how the basic mode of modern learning and education functions. This is the way how a society develops.

Technology, more than its contributions have only reduced and narrowed the human faculty of explorations through the shadows of reality which it creates through multi-dimensional image and graphics. The common people cherish to explore the world with one click of their mouse or tapping of the screen, but have to rely on a truth, on a form of consciousness which is produced by the other. Contemporaneity have forcibly legitimized various ethos of human existence but failed to make it sensible and thus sensitize the people. Due to lack of sensitization people have failed to eternalize the basic optimistic standpoints for social development and changes. And this process of eternalization is only possible when the individuals are once again given back their own socio-cultural and existential elements too which they belong. The concept of non-violence was not a Gandhian discovery but it was a simple effort on behalf of Gandhi to make the people realize to which cults and practices they belong to. Non-violence has often been misread as a metaphor towards helpless sacrifice. But, it has never been so and never will be. The highest level of morality which embosses the simple thoughts of unity, brotherhood or fellow feeling surpasses all forms of current theoretical and philosophical predicaments. Without the basic human values, contemporaneity stands nowhere. It is through these that the globe was constructed and expanded. All forms of advancements and prospective growth came through it. The Layer theory looks forward to create a vast 'salad bowl' of human existence where every forms of individualities and versatilities are carefully nurtured so that the world no more exist on the colonial/vertical plane but on the horizontal plane where the integrated concepts of domination will undergo segregation and hyphenation so that our dream of a pluri-versal, multi-logical society is ultimately transformed into a reality. The centre will be there to hold the structure but it will no more be a representative of monopolist ideology but will be discursive agent through which all forms of voices are individually expressed. Thus let us, obliterate current socio-political cacophonies towards establishing the newly revamped symphonies through unearthing the layers of our existence till the core is reached. The effort must go on.

Works Cited

Arendt, Hannah. (2005). *Essays in Understanding 1930-1954: Formation, Exile and Totalitarianism*, Jerome Kohn (ed.), Schocken Books, New York.

Mignolo, Walter D. (2007). 'Delinking: The rhetoric of modernity, the logic of coloniality and the grammar of de-coloniality', *Cultural Studies* 21(2), pp. 449-514.

Quijano, Anibal. (2007). 'Coloniality and Modernity/Rationality', *Cultural Studies* 21(2), pp. 168-178.

Simpson, Leanne Betasamosake. (2014). 'Land as pedagogy: Nishnaabeg intelligence and rebellious transformation', *Decolonization: Indigeneity, Education and Society* 3(3), pp. 1-25.

Escobar, Arturo. (2007) 'World and Knowledges Otherwise' *Cultural Studies* 21(2), pp. 179-210.

Maldonado-Torres, Nelson. (2007). 'On the Coloniality of Being: Contributions to the development of a Concept', *Cultural Studies* 21(2), pp. 240-270.

Appadurai, Arjun. (1990). 'Disjuncture and Difference in the Global Cultural Economy', *Theory, Culture and Society,* pp. 295-310.

Maturana, Humberto R. (1992). The Tree of Knowledge: The Biological Roots of Human Understanding. Shambhala Publishers.

Duncan, Ronald. (1951). *Selected Writings of Mahatma Gandhi*. Faber and Faber Limited, London.

Richter, Gerhard. (2014). *Afterness: Figures of Following in Modern Though and Aesthetics*. Columbia University Press, New York.

Schmitt, Carl. 2006. The Nomos of the Earth: in the International Law of the Jus Publicum Europaeum, Telos Press Publishing: New York

Alfred, Gerald Taiaiake. 2000. 'Resurgence of Traditional Ways of Being', Simon Ortiz and Labriola Center Lecture, 12 December 2013. [Accessed on 15th April 2015 (https://www.youtube.com/watch?v=3ABP5QhetYs).]

Lyotard, Jean Francois. 1984. The Postmodern Condition. Manchester University Press, United Kingdom.

Desai, Ashwin and Vahed, Goolam. 2015. *The South African Gandhi: Stretcher-Bearer of the Empire*. Navayana Publishing House, New Delhi.

Fanon, Frantz. 2001. *The Wretched of the Earth*. Penguin Publishers, United Kingdom

Sarkar, Swarochish. 2009. *Kavigaan*. Asiatic Society, Bangladesh.

Gikandi, Simon. 2015. 'XIII Theory and Praxis Course Lecture', 30 June. Shillong.

Hobbes, Thomas. 2007. *Leviathan*. Wilder Publications, Radford.

Plato. 2013. *The Republic*. Maple Press, United Kingdom.

De-colonizing the Screen: The Margins Act Back

In the recent times the globe has been debating a lot over the innumerable 'posts' which has been ideologically, bio-graphically and geo-politically enunciated for the sake of defining and re-creating a world beyond the matrices of colonialism or the most current phenomena of coloniality. Unfortunately in most of the cases our effort of disentanglement have proved to be a major failure because our strategies and attitudes have failed to nurture the options which would enable us to think outside the colonial space and untie us from what eminent Argentine de-colonial critic Walter Mignolo terms as 'tyranny of abstract universals.' As a scholar I believe that human expressions forms an integral medium to de-link oneself from the western-centric ideologies as physical and verbal actions forms an integral part of our discourse. The characterization and representation in the Indian movies have undergone consistent ideological and thematic transformations since the last century. The journey has been characterized with multiple contradictions and symbiosis but at the end it has more or less tried ensure the evocation of an Indian version of cinema and cinematography with transcultural and trans-national representations underpinned in it. The empire has written enough to us and it is time for the margins, the colonized, the barbaric representations to act back and my paper will explore the multifaceted ways in which the Indian movies has been fighting hard to dislocate the global/colonial ideologues from its productive sense and its creative lens, inducting the indigenous, native elements in the process.

Introduction: Decolonization

Ramon Grosfoguel, Associate Professor from the University of Berkeley in his essay "A Decolonial Approach to Political-Economy: Transmodernity, Border Thinking and Global Coloniality" analyzes the global socio-epistemic shift since the inception of colonialism in the following manner:

> "We went from the 16th century characterization of 'people without writing' to the 18th and 19th century characterization of 'people without history,' to the 20th century characterization of 'people without development,' and more recently, to the early 21st century of 'people without democracy.' We went from the 16th century 'rights of people' to the 18th century 'rights of man' to the 20th century 'human rights.'"
> (Grosfoguel 7:2009)

The above statements reveal how the juridical face of colonialism have radically modified itself in the 21st century globalism which Peruvian sociologist Anibal Quijano entitles as a system of 'modernity/rationality' (Coloniality and Modernity/Rationality 1:2007). During the 16th century the rise of Eurocentric colonialism, under the canopy of *la mission civilisatrice* (the civilizing mission) and geographical navigations successfully interrupted the global south mostly the Americas, Europeanizing and Latinizing them as what we know as Latin America. Mostly history drafts colonial history in the language of outright physical violence yet its roots lies in the multi-dimensional epistemological and gnoseological constructs which empowered and enabled colonizing powers to reign over the natives.

As we understand the systems and the philosophies of knowledge being imposed upon us it is also very crucial to see how the globe continuously functioned from one version of western centrism to the other and for that we should also invade into the process of commodi-fcation and marketization of the ideologues. According to British social anthropologist John Rankine Goody, the world still lingers within the hellenocentric typologies. In his essay "The Theft of History" (2006) Goody records that the classical antiquities of '*polis*, democracy, freedom, economy, rule of law, art, *logos*' (26-27:2006) continues to reign the world even in the present day. Elaborating his ideas about the 'philosophy of sale' Brazilian law critic Boaventura De Souza Santos in his essay "A Non-Occidentalist West? Learned Ignorance and Ecology of Knowledge" (2009) resorts to the story of "Sale of Creeds" (190:1905) draft-ed by ancient Greek rhetorician and satirist Lucian of Samosata. Zeus along with the assis-tance of Hermes offers various schools of Greek philosophy established by different philoso-phers for the purpose of sale. The 'merchandize' is put on display and every buyer has the right to ask about the value and the contribution of the philosophy in an individual's life be-fore purchasing it. But the philosophies as commodities do not have the rights to question their masters about it. They should function as according to the whims and fancies of their respective masters. This is how the native, indigenous traditions of the Global South and the Far East where trafficked and marketed by the colonizing fathers.

Descartes' *Cogito, Ergo Sum* (I Think, therefore I am) is regarded as the inception point of all modern philosophies and theoretical phraseologies but according to Argentine-Mexican writer and philosopher Enrique Dussel the Descartian cogito map was long preceded by the Eurocentric *Ego Conquiro* (I conquer, therefore I am). It is the philosophy of conquer-ing new lands as already mentioned earlier in the essay which ultimately enabled them to cross and intervene through the borders of other existential disciplines. But modern philoso-phy has consistently failed to locate its locus/loci of enunciations because of its 'point zero' existence as denoted by Columbian Philosopher Santiago Castro-Gomez in the translated version of his essay *"La Hybris del Punto Cero. Ciencia, raza e ilustración en la Nueva Granada (1750-1816)"* (2005). According to him the 'point zero' is the situation which hides the points of inceptions of different strategies and actions this confusing and captivating the colonized natives. This is what led to the creation of the modern version of meta-coloniality as said by Zimbabwean decolonial critic Sabelo Ndlovu-Gatsheni. Gatsheni in his essay "De-coloniality as the Future of Africa" (2015) states that the judicial-political nature of colonialism have withdrawn its institutions long time and has replaced it with the institutions of meta-coloniality which transcends far beyond the physical existence and persist in the realm of abstractness. In order to de-structuralize this realm of abstractness the first thing we should undergo is to come out from the clutches of what Spanish Liberal Philosopher Ortega y Gasset terms as 'orthopedic thinking' (Graham *Theory and History in Ortega y Gasset* 154:2001). I re-structuralize the perspective as 'orthopedic existence.' It is important for us to disenfranchise ourselves from the static clutches of conceptual and analytical thinking. The superfluity and the naturalness of human persistence has to be restored and this is only possible through what eminent Argentine semiotician as 'critical border thinking.' Deriving the term from Chicana thinkers like Gloria Anzaldua (1987) and Jose David Salvidar (1997), Walter Mignolo (2007) through his essay "De-linking" describes that instead of thinking of accessing the centre it is crucial for us to enunciate and emancipate pluri-versal epistemes and pluritopic hermeneutics at the very borders of existence.

In the upcoming section I wish to elaborate the perspective of de-coloniality and border thinking within the contours of arts and aesthetics especially in the arena of the Indian stage and screen performatives.

Decolonizing The Screen

In order to internalize the evolution and the growth of Indian cinema we need to trisect our discussion frame into the following sections:

- The transition of Indian Cinema from the hands of Western techniques, acting and thematic influences towards indigenous socio-cultural, spatio-temporal and eco-political emancipation.
- The pan-Indian and global growth of regional movies and its fragmentation in the hands of pandemic commercialization.
- The influence of Indian theatre forming a backbone in several of the current Indian movies.

A meticulous analysis of the above mentioned points will enable us read Indian movies from a de-colonial perspective. Well commencing with the first point the first light of influence on the Indian movies where thrown by the Lumiere Brothers who in the year 1896 shot their very first movie in Bombay. History took a slightly different turn when Harishchandra Bhatavdekar alias Save Dada, the popular still photographer, largely influenced from the Lumiere Brothers ordered a camera from England and shot a simple wrestling match at the Hanging Gardens which was screened in the year 1899 and is considered to be the first motion picture in the history of Indian cinema.

The first reformation came in the platform of Indian cinema is the production of the silent movie by Dadasaheb Phalke named *Raja Harishchandra* in the year 1913. The silent film was a massive commercial success and it encouraged Dadasaheb to supervise and manage multiple film productions from 1913-1918. It was indeed a tumultuous time in the arena of Indian politics. On one side India is experiencing its struggle for colonial disentanglement from the hands of the Britishers and on the other hand a section of the Indian army has been forcefully christened in the British army to participate in the First World War. Thus it was an extremely difficult time for the practitioners of arts and aesthetics to continue with their creative ventures and it is very much visible in the fragmented situation of Indian cultural productions of that time. Despite this situation the development of Indian movie was a great step ahead which transcended itself from a mere element of thematic and technical mimicry towards re-constituting the lost fragments of Indian history and myths. The welcoming of the Hollywood movies created a special significance in the cultural cauldron of the educated Indian class yet the majority of the population banked on the national and the regional productions that appealed to a larger mass.

The first ever talkie movie directed by Ardeshi Irani was *Alam Ara* in the year 1931. It was another significant break in the Indian cinema and was a very crucial step towards disenfranchising the Indian movies from Eurocentric, hegemonic ideologues. The prospect of decolonizing and pluriversalizing Indian socio-cultural, mythological and historical elements where further encouraged through the development of regional movies. The first Bengali feature film was *Nal Damayanti* produced by J.F. Madan in 1917. In the south the first feature film was *Kechhaka Vadam* which was made by R. Nataraj Mudaliar of Madras. The first Bengali talkie movie was Jamai Sasthi screened in 1931 and was produced by Madan Theatres Limited. Apart from Bengali and South Indian movies there were innumerable productions in Oriya, Punjabi, Gujarati, Marathi and many more. Especially in Marathi *Ayodhyache Raja* was the first talkie that was produced in their respective language in the year 1932. The journey continued unhindered and in a better way after 1947 when prominent directors especially from the segment of Bengali cinema like Satyajit Ray, Bimal Roy and after the 1960s we find a galactic evolution of Ritwik Ghatak, Mrinal Sen and others. Their films thematically ranged from the socio-cultural taboos of dowry, foeticide, patriarchal domination, rural-urban conflict, modern-tradition conflict to the problems and the grievances of the common men and women. What was remarkable was the settings of their movies which mainly remained centered in the hinterland of Indian geography. It was popular step which was hailed pan-globally as it was for the first time that Indian socio-cultural underwent a collective effort to dismantle the 'colonial ideographic approach towards well outlined nomothetics' (Mignolo "Prophets Facing Sidewise" 116:2005) so that the common mass is able to come out of the western-centric, enunciated, generalized and orientalized version of Indian history and myths towards a liberalized, particularized, individualized version of Indian history.

As De Souza Santos in his article "World Social Forum and the Global Left" (2008) mentions that the history as enunciated and emancipated through the colonial discourse has been a specially chosen segment of the native history which satisfies the ethics, typographies and the grammatology of the western ideograph (24). Thus the primary step of decolonization is to identify and excavate the 'past of the past' (De Souza Santos 31) which remains submerged under the uni-ethic and uni-ethnic elements of the western-centric discourses. But the re-creation and re-emergence of the Indian indigenous history and myths through cinema and cinematics have suffered a major setback due to the massive commercialization of Indian cinema which has ultimately evacuated constructive thematic and conceptual propagation and has resorted to blind, dull mimicking of the western themes and most importantly their digital inputs which ensures a smart production output. Digitization of Indian cinema using multi-dimensional, artificial paraphernalia quite successfully bridges the gap between illusion and reality thus deceiving the receptive and analyzing capability of the Indian audience and this element is of great concern. This is not only enslaving Indian cinema within the capitalist entitlement of the "100 Crore Club" but also marginalized the regional movies which cannot incur massive production cost unlike Bollywood.

It is this degradation which ultimately prompted me to formulate the third section which is the conclusion of my essay and it records how theatres has been influencing the Indian cinema in the modern times and its future need to protect its indigenous values.

Conclusion

The commercialization of Indian cinema has caused what Kenyan decolonial critic Ngugi wa Thiong'o terms as 'social decapitation' (Re-membering Africa 65:2009). The root has long term being separated from the body and the connectivity needs to be restored. Recently as an anti-thesis to vibrant commercialism it is being observed that in terms of acting, camera and thematic constructs Indian movies have been following the footsteps of theatre. Even movies like *Oh My God* and *Haider* which has been adapted from a Gujarati play named *Kanji Virudh Kanji* and latter an adaption of Shakespeare's *Hamlet*, has been encrypting multiple theatrical techniques like a play within a play or the musical drama imitating the Dumhal dance of the Wittal Tribe in *Haider*. These are the few instances which represents how Indian movie is transcending from a pure generalized global platform towards the individualized, particularized and most importantly localized versions of expression which were absolutely debarred during the colonial era and current within the ethical persuasion of the comprador bourgeoisie who enjoys the advantage of influencing and imposing the majority with their uni-directional ideological designs. The journey of decolonization has already begun and the margins have enunciated their critical border thinking and have started acting back.

Works Cited

Grosfoguel, Ramon. "A Decolonial Approach to Political-Economy: Transmodernity, Border Thinking and Global Coloniality." *Kult 6 – Special Issue.* Roskilde University, 2009. Print.

Anzaldua, Gloria. *Borderlands/La Frontera: The New Mestiza.* San Francisco: Spinsters Publications, 1987. Print.

Castro-Gomez, Santiago. *La Hybris del Punto Sero. Ciencia, raza e ilustracion en la Nueva Granada (1750-1816).* Bogota: University of Javeriana, 2005. Print.

Saldivar, Jose David. *Border Matters.* Berkeley: University of California Press, 1997. Print.

Santos, Boaventura De Souza. "A Non-Occidentalist West? Learned Ignorance and Ecology of Knowledge." *Theory, Culture and Society, 6(8).* New York: Sage Publishers, 2009. 103-125.

Goody, J. *The Theft of History.* Cambridge: Cambridge University Press, 2006. Print.

Samosata, L. *The Works of Lucian Samosata.* Oxford: Clarendon Press, 1905. Print.

Santos, Boaventuro De Souza. "The World Social Forum and the Global Left." *Politics and Society, 2,* 2008. Print.

Dussel, Enrique. *Beyond Philosophy: Ethics, History, Marxism and Liberation Theology.* New York: Rowman and Littlefield Publishers, 2003. Print.

Mamdani, Mahmood. *Define and Rule: Native As Political Identity.* USA: Harvard University Press, 2012. Print.

Mignolo, Walter D. "Delinking." *Cultural Studies, 21(2).* 2007. Print.

Quijano, Anibal. "Coloniality and Modernity/Rationality." *Cultural Studies, 21(2).* 2007. Print.

Graham, John T. *Theory of History in Ortega y Gasset: The Dawn of Historical Reason.* United States: University of Missouri Press, 1996. Print.

Paul, Sanchita. "History of Indian Cinema." 2005. Web <http://www.mapsofindia.com/myindia/history/history-of-indian-cinema>

YOUR KNOWLEDGE HAS VALUE

- We will publish your bachelor's and
  master's thesis, essays and papers

- Your own eBook and book -
  sold worldwide in all relevant shops

- Earn money with each sale

Upload your text at www.GRIN.com
and publish for free

Lightning Source UK Ltd.
Milton Keynes UK
UKHW040701071122
411784UK00004B/315